The "I Did Us" Concept!

Apostle Paula Ferguson

Published by FOSA Publishing Company, 2024.

THE "I DID US" CONCEPT!

First edition. November 22, 2024.

ISBN: 979-8230395553

Written by Apostle Paula Ferguson.

Also by Apostle Paula Ferguson

Fridge Forks and Fresh Starts: "Building a Healthy Kitchen"
I Just Don't Feel Like It! Finding Motivation When Life Hits Snooze
I Will Understanding Your Divine Calling
Make it Make Sense Recognizing the Move of God in Real Time
The "I Did Us" Concept!

Table of Contents

To my beloved husband, Apostle Craig Ferguson:

Your unwavering love, support, and partnership have been the foundation of my journey. You are my greatest encourager, my steadfast confidant, and my example of grace under pressure. Through every trial and triumph, you have been by my side, reminding me of God's faithfulness and the power of unity.

You are our family's first *I Did Us*. You have faced challenges, endured trials, and paid the price so that we could walk into the blessings and purpose God has prepared for us. Your strength inspires me, your wisdom grounds me, and your love fuels me to continue the work God has placed before us.

Thank you for believing in me, for leading our family with integrity, and for walking this path of purpose hand in hand with me. I honor you, not just as my husband but as a fellow laborer in Christ's kingdom. Together, we are building something eternal.

I love you endlessly.

"The road you walk may be steep, and the fire may burn, but every step you take, every scar you bear, becomes the bridge for someone else to cross. This is the essence of *The 'I Did Us' Concept.*"

About the Author: Apostle Paula Ferguson

Apostle Paula Ferguson is a visionary leader, prolific writer, and transformational teacher whose words resonate with clarity, wisdom, and a deep connection to God's purpose. With decades of ministry experience, she has dedicated her life to guiding others through the complexities of faith, trials, and purpose. Known for her authenticity and unwavering commitment to empowering individuals, Apostle Ferguson has a unique ability to make profound spiritual truths accessible and relatable.

Her writings challenge readers to rise above circumstances, embrace their God-ordained purpose, and live with intentionality. Through her latest work, *I Did Us,* Apostle Ferguson masterfully unpacks the power of legacy, sacrifice, and wisdom, encouraging readers to recognize their role in God's divine plan.

In addition to her work in ministry and writing, she is also the author of the beloved children's series *Out of the Mouth of a Child,* which imparts timeless lessons to younger generations. With every page she writes, Apostle Paula Ferguson continues to leave an indelible mark on hearts and lives, inspiring people to walk boldly into their destinies.

Opening Reflection: The Journey That Makes Us

Life has a way of pulling us through situations that, at first glance, make no sense at all. We set out with plans, dreams, and ambitions, only to find ourselves wandering through battles, setbacks, and silent years that leave us questioning the purpose of it all. It's in these times—when it seems everything is going wrong—that the concept of "I Did Us" begins to take shape.

What does it mean to say "I Did Us"? It's more than just a phrase; it's a declaration of ownership, resilience, and purpose. It means embracing every experience, every triumph, and every struggle as a necessary part of the journey that shapes us. "I Did Us" is the choice to hold onto faith in the unseen purpose behind life's trials, trusting that each one is molding us into someone capable of answering a greater call.

In this second volume of Make It Make Sense, we dive into the idea that our hardships aren't just random obstacles; they're steps in a larger, intentional process. Each challenge, each heartbreak, and each quiet season is shaping us into exactly who we need to be—not only for ourselves but for others. You are being prepared, refined, and equipped because you are somebody's answer. You are somebody's "I Did Us."

The Purpose Behind the Pain

When we think of purpose, we often think about success, fulfillment, and joy. But purpose rarely arrives without a period of preparation—sometimes preparation that looks nothing like what we expected or even wanted. The story of Joseph in the Bible gives us a perfect example. As a young man, Joseph had dreams of greatness, but those dreams quickly took a detour. He was betrayed by his own brothers, sold into slavery, and later thrown into prison for a crime he didn't commit. Yet through it all, there was a recurring theme: "The Lord was with him."

Joseph's journey didn't make sense at first. He had moments where he was far from the life he'd imagined, seemingly abandoned in foreign lands, forgotten in a prison cell. But what he didn't realize was that each step was a layer of preparation. Each hardship added a new skill, a new level of resilience, and a new depth to his character. The skills he learned in his father's house as a young man were amplified in Egypt, first as a slave in Potiphar's house and then as a prisoner. In both places, Joseph grew in responsibility and wisdom, until finally, he was ready to step into his destiny as a leader who would save a nation.

In the same way, the trials we face today are often unseen preparations for our future. They may not look like growth from the outside, but each hardship is equipping us with skills, character, and faith that we'll need down the road. When we say "I Did Us," we're claiming every bit of that process. We're recognizing that nothing in our lives is wasted, that each piece—no matter how painful—has a purpose.

The Transformative Power of Resilience

Resilience isn't built on smooth roads; it's forged in storms. "I Did Us" is about looking back at those storms and saying, "I see it now. I needed that." It's about choosing to see purpose even in pain and trusting that, through it all, we're being shaped into people who can make a difference.

Many of us will face a period of waiting or isolation, a time when it seems like nothing is happening, much like Joseph's silent years in prison. These moments can feel like abandonment, but they're often the times when God is closest, working on our hearts and strengthening our spirits. These are the silent seasons that teach us humility, trust, and endurance. They allow us to confront ourselves, letting go of bitterness, impatience, or fear that might otherwise sabotage our future.

When we look back, we'll see that every struggle was a stepping stone. Each painful experience was a piece of training, molding us into someone with the wisdom, patience, and strength to step into the rooms we were always meant to enter.

The Call to Be Somebody's Answer

As we move through this book, I want you to see yourself as more than just a survivor of your own battles. I want you to see that you are somebody's answer. You are somebody's "I Did Us." Just as Joseph's story didn't end in a prison cell, neither does yours. Every hardship, every moment of resilience, every lesson learned has prepared you to be the solution to a problem, the answer to a need, the support for someone else's journey.

When Joseph finally stood before Pharaoh, he was ready because he had allowed every part of his journey to shape him. His pain had refined him, his patience had humbled him, and his faith had strengthened him. He didn't have to pretend to be something he wasn't his journey had already prepared him for that moment. Pharaoh saw his authenticity, his wisdom, and his integrity, and Joseph became the leader he was always meant to be.

In the same way, your journey, everything you've been through—is preparing you to be that answer for someone. Whether it's in your family, your community, your business, or your ministry, your experiences are setting you up to walk into a room and say, "I know what needs to be done here. I have the answer."

Owning Your "I Did Us"

As we embark on this journey through Make It Make Sense: I Did Us, remember that this is about embracing the fullness of your life—its trials, its triumphs, and its purpose. When you say "I Did Us," you're not just speaking about your past; you're claiming the strength, the resilience, and the wisdom you've gained as tools for your future.

Let this book be a guide to seeing yourself as someone uniquely prepared, someone who has endured storms and emerged with a purpose. Let it remind you that nothing in your life is wasted, and every experience is working together to prepare you for a greater role.

Through these chapters, we'll explore how to embrace every piece of the journey, even the painful ones, as part of a divine preparation. We'll see how our struggles, our silent years, and our moments of resilience equip us to be a solution for others. When the time comes, you'll be ready to step into your moment with clarity and purpose, saying, "I did this, I am prepared, and I am here for a reason."

Let's begin this journey of making it make sense. Together, let's find the purpose in the process, the power in the preparation, and the strength to say, with confidence and faith, I Did Us.

Chapter 1: Hardship as Preparation – You Are Somebody's "I Did Us"

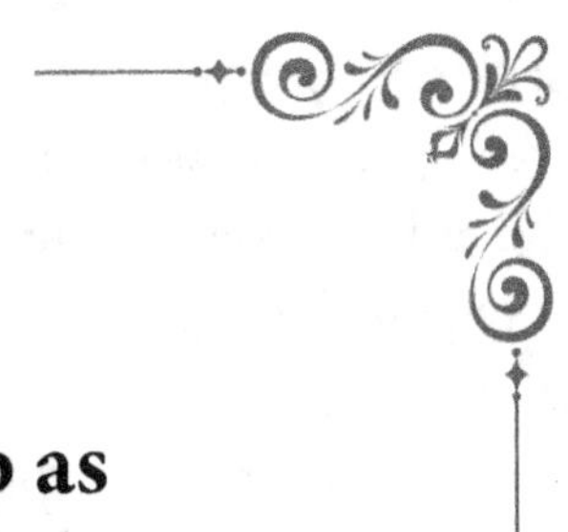

When life seems to be an endless series of battles, it's natural to ask, Why am I going through this? Why do I have to pay this price, face this struggle, endure this loss? These are questions that echo in the hearts of people who feel weighed down by trials. But the answer to these questions, as hard as it is to accept at times, may lie in the very people who will one day walk into your life seeking the exact wisdom and experience you've gained through those battles.

You are not merely a survivor of your hardships. You are being shaped to become someone else's answer. You are somebody's "I Did Us."

The Purpose of Paying the Price

Imagine you've spent years pursuing a dream, investing money, time, and effort, only to feel like you're continually falling short. Perhaps you've emptied your bank account to finance a business that struggled to take off. Maybe you've faced job loss, lost relationships, or sacrificed your personal life along the way. It's natural to feel like these sacrifices might be wasted. But what if they aren't wasted at all? What if these sacrifices are part of a larger purpose?

The experiences we pay for in tears, lost resources, and countless hours are investments in wisdom that will one day be a lifeline for someone else. Think of it this way: every time you've learned what doesn't work, every time you've had to start over, you were gathering knowledge that you can share. The mistakes and setbacks you've endured become a map for someone else who's just starting on a similar path. You paid the price, so they don't have to.

Consider Thomas Edison. Known for his persistence, he famously tested thousands of different materials and configurations in his quest to create a working lightbulb. When asked how it felt to have failed so many times, Edison is said to have responded, "I have not failed. I've just found 10,000 ways that won't work." Edison's story is a reminder that each apparent failure is a learning step. What he discovered during those thousands of attempts was not wasted effort; it became knowledge that paved the way for others who would build upon his work.

Similarly, the hardships you endure and the lessons you learn are not just for you. They are for the benefit of others who will one day ask you for guidance, for the wisdom you alone have gained. When they come to you and say, "How did you get through this? How did you know which way to go?" you will be able to respond, not with abstract advice, but with hard-earned knowledge from your own life.

Training for Purpose: The Doctor's Journey

Another example of this principle is found in the journey of a medical student. From the moment they enter medical school, future doctors begin a path of rigorous study, long hours, and countless sacrifices. They miss out on social gatherings, endure sleepless nights, and pour over textbooks and research papers until their eyes are weary. Why? Not because it's easy, and certainly not for personal pleasure, but because each step is essential preparation for the moment a patient sits down in front of them and says, "Doc, I'm in pain."

When a patient describes a symptom, a doctor doesn't guess blindly. Years of study and experience have trained the doctor to recognize patterns, to understand that pain in one area of the body may actually be caused by an issue somewhere else entirely. The doctor's hard-earned knowledge allows them to say, "Your leg pain is caused by an issue with your hip." The years of sacrifice pay off because now the doctor has the wisdom to provide the right answer.

In the same way, each of us is being prepared for moments when someone will come to us, seeking answers. When you face setbacks and struggles, when you learn through trial and error, you're building a knowledge base. You're becoming the "doctor" in a specific area of life, someone with the insight needed to guide others. You may not have known it at the time, but each hardship was preparing you to be the person who could say, "Here's what you need to know. Here's what I learned the hard way, so you don't have to go through the same."

Choosing Perspective: Finding Value in Hardship

What separates those who crumble under hardship from those who rise above it is often a matter of perspective. When you encounter obstacles, the way you view them can transform how you experience them. Seeing setbacks as purposeful rather than pointless can shift your entire journey.

Perspective is what turned Thomas Edison's thousands of failed attempts into a victory. He didn't see those thousands of tries as wasted time; he saw them as essential steps toward success. Similarly, viewing our own challenges as necessary parts of our preparation can give us strength. Rather than asking, "Why me?" we can begin to ask, "What can I learn from this?"

Our perspective doesn't eliminate pain or make hardships easier, but it does allow us to find purpose in them. Every hardship becomes part of our preparation. When we adopt this mindset, we start to see our struggles as qualifications, as experiences that are equipping us to be the answer someone else will need.

Embracing the Role of "I Did Us"

Imagine a friend or a family member comes to you, struggling with something you've faced before. They ask for advice, looking to you for guidance and insight. In that moment, you realize that everything you went through wasn't just for you—it was for them too. Because of what you endured, you now have the experience to guide them in ways that only you can.

Each one of us has unique experiences that make us somebody's "I Did Us." You are somebody's answer. There will be people who come into your life, who find themselves in situations similar to what you've already overcome. They won't have to make the same mistakes, pay the same price, or endure the same losses, because you've already done it. You've paid the price and walked the road, and now you can provide them with insight, wisdom, and hope.

When we view ourselves as somebody's "I Did Us," our struggles become more than personal challenges. They become preparation, training us to stand in the gap for others, to be a source of guidance and support.

Seeing Jesus as the Ultimate "I Did Us"

There is no greater example of someone being a sacrificial answer than Jesus Christ. Jesus bore the ultimate burden, paying the highest price so that humanity wouldn't have to bear it alone. Isaiah 53:5 reminds us, "But he was wounded for our transgressions, he was bruised for our iniquities: the chastisement of our peace was upon him; and with his stripes we are healed." Jesus endured suffering, pain, and sacrifice not because He needed it for Himself, but because we did.

When we consider Christ's sacrifice, we see the ultimate act of being somebody's "I Did Us." He faced rejection, humiliation, and death, carrying the weight of humanity's sin so that we could find freedom, peace, and hope. Jesus didn't have to go through what He did, but He chose to, knowing that His suffering would pave the way for countless lives to find redemption. He is the ultimate example of someone who endured hardship for the sake of others.

In our own lives, we are called to follow this example, to endure trials with the knowledge that our pain can bring healing, guidance, and hope to others. We may not be asked to bear the weight of the world, but we are each asked to use our experiences to help those around us.

Don't Give Up—Your Purpose is Bigger Than You

As you go through challenges and hardships, remember that they are not without purpose. Each trial, each lesson learned, each sacrifice is preparing you to be the answer to someone's need. You are being positioned to be somebody's "I Did Us." It might not make sense right now, and the price might feel heavy, but your experiences are equipping you with something invaluable: the wisdom, perspective, and resilience that someone else will one day need.

So, when you feel like giving up, remind yourself that your journey isn't just for you. It's for the people who will come into your life looking for answers. It's for those who need someone to stand before them and say, "I've been there. I've done that. I paid the price so you don't have to."

Each struggle, each setback, and each success is shaping you into the person you're meant to be—not just for yourself, but for others. Embrace your journey, knowing that you are being prepared for a greater purpose. You are being positioned to become someone's answer, to be their "I Did Us," and that purpose gives meaning to every step of your journey.

Chapter 2: Positioned for a Greater Purpose – Joseph's Story

In life, we often face hardships that seem unfair, even unbearable. We endure betrayal, rejection, and loneliness, wondering why we have to go through so much. But sometimes, these trials are part of a divine setup. They're preparing us and positioning us to fulfill a purpose greater than ourselves. Joseph's story is a profound example of how trials can position us for impact. Through everything he faced, Joseph was being prepared to be the solution not only for his family but for an entire nation.

From Privilege to the Pit

Joseph's life began with privilege. As the favored son of Jacob, he was given a beautiful, colorful coat—a symbol of his father's love and perhaps a sign of his future potential. Joseph also had dreams, visions from God that one day he would rise to a place of prominence. In these dreams, his family members were bowing to him, hinting at a future where he would hold a significant position. But Joseph's journey to that place of influence was not a straight line. In fact, it took him through some of the darkest places imaginable.

Joseph's brothers resented him for his favored status and his dreams, seeing him as arrogant and naive. Their jealousy grew until they conspired to get rid of him. They threw him into a pit and then sold him to a caravan of traders heading to Egypt. In an instant, Joseph's life was turned upside down. He went from being the cherished son in his father's house to a slave in a foreign land.

Imagine the shock and betrayal Joseph must have felt. One moment he was the beloved son, and the next, he was alone, a stranger in a strange land. It would have been easy for Joseph to give up, to feel abandoned by God and believe his life was ruined. But as we'll see, each step in Joseph's journey was a piece of a greater plan.

Learning Through Service in Potiphar's House

After being sold into slavery, Joseph ended up in the house of Potiphar, an officer of Pharaoh and captain of the guard. Though he was now a servant, Joseph didn't let bitterness take root. Instead, he chose to work diligently and faithfully, making the best of his situation. Genesis 39:2-4 says, "The Lord was with Joseph so that he prospered, and he lived in the house of his Egyptian master. When his master saw that the Lord was with him and that the Lord gave him success in everything he did, Joseph found favor in his eyes and became his attendant."

In Potiphar's house, Joseph's work ethic and integrity became apparent. Potiphar trusted him so much that he placed Joseph in charge of his entire household. Joseph was learning valuable skills—how to manage people, resources, and responsibilities—that would later become essential in his role as a leader. These skills weren't developed in a palace but in a position of servitude. Sometimes, God uses places of humility to develop the very qualities we need to step into our purpose.

Joseph's time in Potiphar's house reminds us that even when we're not where we want to be, we can still grow and learn. We can still serve with excellence. Joseph's work in Potiphar's house was preparation, positioning him for the greater purpose that lay ahead. In our own lives, we often find ourselves in "Potiphar's house"—places we didn't choose, jobs that seem beneath our abilities, situations that feel restrictive. But it's in these places that God can shape us, teaching us lessons we'll need in the future.

A Test of Integrity and the Path to Prison

Joseph's faithfulness in Potiphar's house didn't go unnoticed. Potiphar's wife, attracted to Joseph, tried to seduce him. But Joseph refused her advances, saying, "How then could I do such a wicked thing and sin against God?" (Genesis 39:9). Joseph's response shows his unwavering commitment to his values, even when no one else was watching. He knew that his integrity was worth more than any temporary pleasure or gain.

However, Potiphar's wife falsely accused Joseph of assault, and he was thrown into prison. Once again, Joseph's life took a drastic and seemingly unfair turn. He had done the right thing, yet he found himself in an even worse situation. It would have been easy for him to question God, to wonder why he was facing such injustice when he had tried to live honorably. But Joseph's imprisonment was not the end of his story; it was another step in his preparation.

In prison, Joseph continued to live with integrity. The prison warden noticed his character and eventually placed Joseph in charge of all the prisoners. Even in this dark place, Joseph's faithfulness and resilience shone through. He didn't let his circumstances define him; instead, he allowed his character to guide his actions.

Sometimes, life's greatest tests come when we feel we're at our lowest. In these moments, it's tempting to compromise or let bitterness take over. But Joseph's story shows us that holding onto integrity, even in the darkest times, is essential. These moments of testing refine us, shaping us into people who can handle greater responsibilities.

Divine Appointments in Unexpected Places

Joseph's time in prison was not without purpose. While he was there, he met two of Pharaoh's officials—the chief cupbearer and the chief baker—who had been imprisoned. One night, each of these men had a troubling dream, and Joseph, seeing their distress, offered to interpret the dreams through God's guidance. He accurately interpreted their dreams, predicting the cupbearer's release and the baker's death.

Joseph's encounter with these officials was no coincidence. Though he didn't know it at the time, his willingness to serve and help them would eventually open the door to his freedom and his ultimate purpose. Joseph asked the cupbearer to remember him once he was released, hoping for an opportunity to be freed from prison. Yet, the cupbearer forgot about Joseph, leaving him to wait in prison for two more years.

These years in prison were a time of silence and waiting, a season where it seemed nothing was happening. But in reality, Joseph was being prepared, refined, and positioned. It was a time of internal growth, where he learned to rely on God fully, even when his circumstances seemed hopeless.

In our lives, we often find ourselves in seasons of waiting, wondering if we've been forgotten or abandoned. But these seasons are not wasted. They are times of preparation, times when God is working on our hearts, shaping us to step into the purpose He has planned. Like Joseph, we may not see the purpose of our waiting, but we can trust that God is positioning us for something greater.

Positioned to Save a Nation

Two years later, Pharaoh had a pair of disturbing dreams that none of his advisors could interpret. It was then that the cupbearer remembered Joseph and mentioned him to Pharaoh. Joseph was quickly brought before Pharaoh, and through God's wisdom, he interpreted the dreams, explaining that Egypt would face seven years of abundance followed by seven years of severe famine. Joseph advised Pharaoh on how to prepare for the famine, proposing a plan to store grain during the years of abundance.

Pharaoh recognized the wisdom in Joseph's words and appointed him as second-in-command over all of Egypt, saying, "Can we find anyone like this man, one in whom is the spirit of God?" (Genesis 41:38). In an instant, Joseph was elevated from prisoner to governor, positioned to save Egypt and many surrounding nations from starvation.

Every step of Joseph's journey—the betrayal, the slavery, the prison—had positioned him to step into this role. Had he not been in Egypt, had he not served in Potiphar's house or met the cupbearer in prison, he wouldn't have been able to interpret Pharaoh's dream and offer a plan to save the nation. Each hardship had prepared him to be the answer to a crisis that threatened countless lives.

Joseph's story reminds us that God's purpose often requires us to go through challenges we wouldn't choose for ourselves. These hardships are part of the preparation and positioning that allow us to step into roles where we can make a difference. Joseph's journey encourages us to trust that even in our most difficult seasons, God is at work, aligning our path with His purpose.

You Are Positioned for a Greater Purpose

Joseph's story is not just about survival; it's about positioning. Each trial he endured prepared him to be the answer to a future crisis. In the same way, the challenges you face, the setbacks and disappointments, are not in vain. They are positioning you for a greater purpose.

There will be people who come into your life, seeking answers that only you can provide. Your experiences, your perseverance, your faithfulness will equip you to guide others, to offer wisdom and support that comes from a place of understanding. You are being positioned to be somebody's "I Did Us," someone who can stand in the gap and say, "I've been there. I've walked that path, and I know the way through."

When life takes you through unexpected places, remember that you are being positioned for something greater. Just as Joseph's journey prepared him to be the answer for his family and an entire nation, your journey is preparing you to be the answer for someone else. Embrace each season, knowing that you are being shaped, refined, and positioned to fulfill a purpose beyond yourself.

Chapter 3: Refined Through Trials – Becoming the Solution

Embracing Loss as Part of the Process

Ruth's story begins in the ashes of loss. A young Moabite woman who had married into a Jewish family, Ruth found herself grieving the death of her husband. Her mother-in-law, Naomi, was also devastated, having lost not only her husband but also both of her sons, including Ruth's husband. Naomi's grief was so deep that she renamed herself "Mara," meaning "bitter," saying, "The Almighty has made my life very bitter" (Ruth 1:20).

Despite her grief and bitterness, Naomi still held wisdom and insight that Ruth would one day need. Ruth chose to stay with her, making a bold declaration: "Where you go, I will go, and where you stay, I will stay. Your people will be my people and your God my God" (Ruth 1:16). Ruth committed herself to follow Naomi, embracing a path she didn't fully understand. But had Ruth not made this choice—had she chosen to stay in Moab rather than journeying to Bethlehem with Naomi—she would have missed her purpose.

Recognizing the Significance of Difficult Relationships

Naomi may have appeared bitter and broken, yet her role in Ruth's life was critical. Though she was hurting, Naomi still held keys to Ruth's future. She understood the customs of Israel and knew how to navigate the social and cultural challenges Ruth would face as a foreigner. Naomi's experiences, even her pain, gave her a unique perspective that Ruth would need to reach her destiny.

Sometimes, the people God places in our lives don't look like ideal mentors or guides. They may be grieving, bitter, or wrestling with their own struggles. But even in their brokenness, God can use them to impart the wisdom we need. Naomi, in all her pain and bitterness, became Ruth's "I Did Us." She was the answer Ruth needed, directing her toward choices that would change both their lives.

When we encounter people like Naomi, we may feel tempted to judge them or distance ourselves. But these "Naomis" may hold wisdom and direction that are essential to our journey. Naomi guided Ruth with an understanding that could only come from having lived through her own trials. Ruth's loyalty to Naomi, even when Naomi seemed disillusioned and discouraged, positioned her to receive the guidance that would lead her to her purpose.

Serving Under Someone Who Feels "Less Qualified"

By all appearances, Ruth could have felt she deserved more than what Naomi had to offer. Naomi's bitterness and grief could have made her seem like an unlikely guide. Yet Ruth remained humble, willing to follow Naomi's lead even though it meant serving and learning from someone who felt abandoned and bitter.

In our own lives, God may call us to serve under people who are imperfect, who seem "less qualified" or "less capable." They may struggle with their own issues or have shortcomings that make it difficult to learn from them. But God can still use these individuals to impart something important, something we wouldn't gain elsewhere. Ruth chose to remain with Naomi, trusting that even if Naomi was broken and bitter, there was still wisdom to glean. Sometimes, God places us under those who are struggling or imperfect so that we can learn valuable lessons, even from their pain or mistakes.

Divine Purpose Through Obedience

Ruth's choice to follow Naomi was not just about companionship or loyalty; it was part of a divine setup. In the spiritual "scrolls" of Ruth's life—God's divine plan for her—it was written that she would leave her home in Moab and journey to Bethlehem, where she would fulfill her purpose. Her obedience to follow Naomi, despite her bitterness, was part of a greater calling.

Ruth's willingness to stay with Naomi positioned her in the lineage of Jesus Christ. Her marriage to Boaz placed her in the line that would lead to Jesse, the father of King David, and eventually to Jesus Himself. In choosing to follow Naomi, Ruth became an essential part of God's plan to bring redemption to the world. She was positioned not only to bless Naomi's life but to play a role in God's plan for all of humanity.

In the same way, our choices to serve, obey, and remain faithful even when it's difficult can position us within God's plan. Sometimes, we don't see the full impact of our actions or the generations that will be blessed through our choices. Ruth was somebody's "I Did Us" for every believer, every child of God who would one day come to know Jesus Christ. Her obedience brought her into a legacy that would impact lives beyond anything she could have imagined.

The Humbling Path of Gleaning in the Fields

Ruth's journey also brought her to a place of humility. In Bethlehem, she took on the task of gleaning in the fields—gathering leftover grain after the harvesters had finished. This was work reserved for the poor and marginalized. Ruth, who could have felt entitled to more, humbled herself to gather scraps in a foreign land.

Her choice to work humbly and diligently placed her in the field of Boaz, a man of integrity who would eventually become her husband. This wasn't a coincidence; God arranged for Ruth to be seen by Boaz because of her faithfulness in serving humbly. Boaz noticed Ruth's dedication, her loyalty to Naomi, and her resilience, and he extended kindness and protection to her.

Sometimes, we find ourselves in seasons where we feel we are "gleaning in the fields"—doing work that feels beneath us or enduring circumstances we believe we don't deserve. But these humble places are often where God positions us for divine appointments. Our willingness to serve humbly and faithfully positions us to receive blessings and opportunities that only God could arrange.

Divine Encounters in Humble Places

When Ruth encountered Boaz, she couldn't have known that he would be the one to redeem her and Naomi's family. But her willingness to glean in his field, her humble obedience, opened the door to a future that was beyond her imagination. Boaz recognized the qualities that God had refined in Ruth through her trials, and he extended favor to her because of it.

In our lives, we too may encounter people who recognize the qualities that God has shaped within us. When we serve humbly and live faithfully, God notices, and He arranges encounters with those who can open doors for us. Ruth's encounter with Boaz wasn't just about immediate provision; it was about positioning her in God's redemptive plan.

Recognizing the Legacy of Obedience

Ruth's marriage to Boaz wasn't just a personal blessing. It placed her in the lineage of King David and, ultimately, Jesus Christ. Through her obedience and faithfulness, Ruth became part of a legacy that would bless generations to come. She became somebody's "I Did Us" for every child of God, every believer in Christ. Her life and choices were woven into God's plan to bring redemption and salvation to humanity.

Ruth's story reminds us that our trials, sacrifices, and acts of obedience are often part of a much larger picture. The people we choose to serve, the humility we embrace, and the willingness to follow even when it's difficult are all part of a divine legacy. We may not see the full impact, but God is using our lives to bless and prepare future generations. Just as Ruth's life paved the way for the birth of Jesus, our lives can pave the way for others to encounter God's grace and purpose.

Becoming the Solution Through Refinement

Ruth's journey shows us that becoming somebody's "I Did Us" often involves a process of loss, humility, and obedience. She served Naomi, despite her bitterness, and followed her to a new land, embracing a path of faithfulness and dedication. Through her trials, Ruth was refined and conditioned to fit into the destiny God had for her. She became the solution, not only for Naomi but for generations to come.

As we reflect on Ruth's story, we're reminded that our own lives are part of a divine setup. We're being refined, prepared, and positioned to be the answer for someone else. Whether we're serving under a Naomi, gleaning in a field, or humbling ourselves in ways we never anticipated, God is using each step to prepare us for our purpose.

Sometimes, our "I Did Us" journey means serving people who are struggling, learning from those who are imperfect, and embracing opportunities for humility. Each challenge, each act of obedience, is preparing us to be the answer that someone else needs. So, when you feel overlooked, when you're serving under someone who is broken or bitter, or when you're doing work that feels beneath you, remember Ruth's story. Remember that you are being positioned for a greater purpose, refined to become the solution, and prepared to be somebody's "I Did Us."

Chapter 4: The Ultimate "I Did Us" – The Sacrifice of Christ

A Heart That Knows Its Purpose

When Jesus came to earth, He knew the depth of His mission. He came to save a world that didn't know it needed saving, to heal hearts that would reject Him, and to serve people who would ultimately betray, deny, and abandon Him. Yet, despite knowing what lay ahead, He walked a path of obedience, sacrifice, and love. He carried in His heart the knowledge that every act, every step, and every word would lead to the cross. His sacrifice was not only physical; it was a complete surrender of His life, His will, and His very existence for the sake of others.

Jesus understood the hearts of those He was sent to serve. He saw beyond their words and outward actions, perceiving their motives, doubts, and fears. He knew that some of those closest to Him would betray Him. Yet, He loved them fully. John 2:24-25 tells us, "But Jesus would not entrust himself to them, for he knew all people. He did not need any testimony about mankind, for he knew what was in each person." This insight into human hearts was both a gift and a burden. Jesus saw the brokenness and resistance in people, yet He continued to pour out His love, knowing they might never understand or reciprocate.

Purchased Knowledge: The Price of Experience

Jesus' journey was one of "purchased sense," a concept that reflects how wisdom and knowledge come through experience. Jesus' path to the cross was not just about enduring physical pain; it was about gaining the deep, embodied understanding of human suffering, sin, and weakness. He walked among us, experiencing our limitations, temptations, and heartbreaks. This "bought sense" became the foundation of His empathy and intercession on our behalf. Because

He lived as one of us, He intimately understands our struggles, and His sacrifice holds the power to heal us fully.

In life, we often find that purchased knowledge—knowledge gained through personal experience and sacrifice—is the most valuable and transformative. Once we've paid a price for wisdom, no one can take it from us. It's ours. We've walked the road, paid the cost, and learned the lessons firsthand. Jesus, in His humanity, paid the ultimate price, gaining a knowledge of our condition that was written in His heart and body. Hebrews 4:15 reminds us, "For we do not have a high priest who is unable to empathize with our weaknesses, but we have one who has been tempted in every way, just as we are—yet he did not sin." His sacrifice is the ultimate example of what it means to carry knowledge that can change others' lives.

Knowing Betrayal and Serving Anyway

Among the people Jesus chose to serve was Judas Iscariot, a man He knew would betray Him. Judas's betrayal was not a surprise to Jesus; it was part of the divine plan. In John 6:70-71, Jesus even says, "Have I not chosen you, the Twelve? Yet one of you is a devil!" Jesus knew Judas's heart from the beginning, yet He still selected him, knowing that Judas's betrayal would lead to the fulfillment of His mission.

This part of Jesus' journey teaches us that sometimes, we are called to serve alongside people who are not for us, people who might harm or betray us. It's painful, but God can use even these relationships to position us for our purpose. Just as Judas was "chosen" for a specific role, sometimes people are positioned in our lives not to support us, but to refine us and ultimately propel us toward our destiny. They may hurt us, oppose us, or even work against us, but in God's sovereignty, their actions are woven into His larger plan for our lives.

In the same way, there may be people in our lives who seem anointed to test us or betray us, yet they serve a purpose in our journey. Jesus knew Judas's heart, but He still washed his feet and broke bread with him, fully aware of what Judas would do. This is sacrificial love in its purest form—loving, serving, and giving without expectation, even when betrayal is certain.

The Silence of Sacrifice

As Jesus moved closer to the cross, He faced unimaginable trials. He was falsely accused, mocked, and beaten. People hurled insults at Him, and yet, He remained silent. Isaiah 53:7 prophesied this about Jesus: "He was oppressed and afflicted, yet he did not open his mouth; he was led like a lamb to the slaughter, and as a sheep before its shearers is silent, so he did not open his mouth."

The silence of Jesus during His suffering is a powerful example for us. Sometimes, our sacrifice requires us to bear insults, accusations, and misunderstandings without defending ourselves. Jesus could have justified Himself, proven His innocence, or called down legions of angels to rescue Him. But He chose silence, surrendering His right to defend Himself. His silence was an act of ultimate trust in the Father's plan, a submission to the greater purpose for which He was sent.

In our lives, there will be times when sacrifice requires silence. When we are misunderstood, falsely accused, or rejected, we may feel the urge to explain or justify ourselves. But sometimes, God calls us to endure in silence, trusting that He sees and knows the truth. Jesus' silent suffering reminds us that not every battle needs to be fought with words. Sometimes, the most powerful testimony we can give is to endure faithfully and let God be our defender.

The Depth of His Love for Those Who Wouldn't Love Him Back

Jesus loved deeply, even knowing that many would never love Him in return. He healed the sick, fed the hungry, and taught the crowds, fully aware that some of those same people would later cry out for His crucifixion. Jesus was willing to serve, heal, and love people who would never understand or honor His sacrifice. This is a challenging truth for us to accept—that we may be called to serve people who don't appreciate us, to love those who will never love us back, and to give to those who may never reciprocate.

Jesus' love was not conditional. He didn't come only for those who would accept Him; He came for everyone, even those who would reject Him. This radical love is the essence of His sacrifice. Romans 5:8 says, "But God demonstrates his own love for us in this: While we were still sinners, Christ died for us." Jesus' love reached across time, embracing the hearts of those who would come to Him as well as those who would turn away.

This kind of love challenges us to go beyond ourselves, to serve and love people even when we know they may never appreciate or return that love. Jesus' sacrifice teaches us that true love gives without expecting anything in return. When we serve, give, and sacrifice for others, we embody the love of Christ, knowing that it may never be reciprocated or even acknowledged.

The Sacrifice of Knowing the End Yet Walking the Path

Perhaps one of the most challenging aspects of Jesus' sacrifice was knowing the ending yet still walking the path. He was fully aware of the suffering, betrayal, and agony that awaited Him, yet He didn't waver. In the Garden of Gethsemane, He prayed, "My Father, if it is possible, may this cup be taken from me. Yet not as I will, but as you will" (Matthew 26:39). His humanity wrestled with the weight of what lay ahead, yet He chose obedience, surrendering His will to the Father's plan.

Jesus knew that His road would lead to the cross, but He walked it anyway. He knew the pain, yet He embraced it for our sake. This willingness to walk a path of suffering for the benefit of others is the ultimate "I Did Us." Jesus' sacrifice was not forced; it was a choice, an act of love that reached across eternity to redeem humanity.

In our own lives, we may be called to walk paths we wouldn't choose, to endure hardships we'd rather avoid. But Jesus' journey teaches us that sometimes, our greatest impact comes through obedience to a difficult path. When we embrace God's plan, even when it includes suffering, we align ourselves with His purpose, knowing that our sacrifice is part of a larger story.

Completing the Ultimate "I Did Us" on the Cross

On the cross, Jesus completed His ultimate act of sacrifice. Bearing the weight of humanity's sins, He cried out, "It is finished" (John 19:30). In that moment, the price was paid, the sacrifice was complete, and the pathway to redemption was opened for all who would believe. Jesus' sacrifice didn't end with His suffering; it culminated in victory. His resurrection was the final proof that His sacrifice was sufficient, that He had overcome sin and death.

Jesus' "I Did Us" was for all of humanity, reaching into every heart and every generation. He paid the ultimate price so that we could find life, hope, and freedom. His sacrifice reminds us that even when the road is hard, even when the cost is high, there is a greater purpose at work. Jesus' journey from the manger to the cross teaches us that true love sacrifices without reservation, and true purpose often requires laying down our lives for others.

Following the Example of the Ultimate Sacrifice

As we reflect on Jesus' journey, we are reminded that we, too, are called to sacrifice. We are called to serve, to love, and to give, even when it isn't easy or appreciated. We may have to walk paths of difficulty, endure misunderstandings, or love people who won't love us back. But when we do, we follow the example of the One who made the ultimate sacrifice.

Jesus was, and is, the ultimate "I Did Us." His life was given for our sake, His love poured out without limit. And as we walk in His footsteps, we, too, become answers for those around us. We may be called to make sacrifices, to endure hardships, and to walk paths that aren't easy. But in doing so, we carry forward the legacy of the One who laid down His life so that we could truly live.

Chapter 5: Breaking Free from Past Limits – Embracing Growth Through the Legacy of "I Did Us"

<u>I</u>ntroduction: From Glory to Glory Through "I Did Us"

The Bible tells us we are transformed from "glory to glory" (2 Corinthians 3:18), moving through stages of growth, purpose, and transformation. Each stage calls us to step into a deeper understanding of God's plan for our lives, often stretching us beyond our comfort zones. But we don't travel this journey alone. The sacrifices and wisdom of others—the *I Did Us* figures in our lives—form the foundation that allows us to embrace our next level. They've walked this road, faced the flames, and endured the challenges so that we can step forward with clarity and confidence.

Breaking free from past limits is essential to fulfilling our God-ordained destiny. But this process requires us to release old habits, outdated mindsets, and familiar comforts. Like a baby leaving the womb or a child learning to walk, each stage of growth pushes us into the unknown. The *I Did Us* voices in our lives are there to guide us, offering wisdom born from experience. They remind us that growth is not just about letting go but about stepping forward into the greater purpose God has prepared.

The Path of Growth: Leaving the Past Behind

Every stage of growth begins with a departure. When a baby is born, it leaves the womb—the only world it has ever known. This transition, though necessary for life, is marked by separation and discomfort. Similarly, when God calls us to grow, He often requires us to leave behind what is familiar and step into something entirely new. This can feel unsettling, but it is an essential part of the process.

The *"I Did Us"* figures in our lives have already navigated these transitions. They've faced the discomfort of leaving behind their own past limitations and stepped into the unknown with faith. Their journeys show us that growth requires trust, courage, and the willingness to let go of what no longer serves God's purpose in our lives. By leaning on their wisdom, we gain the strength to move forward.

This legacy of guidance reminds us that growth is not a solitary endeavor. Just as a child is taught to walk, we are often guided by the experiences of those who've gone before us. Their scars and stories become the roadmap that helps us navigate our own journey. They remind us that while leaving the past can be painful, it's a necessary step toward embracing the future God has prepared.

Overcoming Nostalgia: The Trap of Looking Back

Nostalgia can be both a comfort and a trap. It's natural to reflect on where we've come from, but when nostalgia holds us back, it becomes a hindrance to growth. Like the Israelites longing for Egypt, we can sometimes cling to past seasons, even when God is calling us to something greater. The *"I Did Us"* voices remind us that the past is a reference point, not a resting place.

Hebrews 6:5 speaks of "tasting the powers of the age to come," giving us glimpses of the future God has prepared. These glimpses are meant to stir our faith, urging us to press forward with courage. Those who say, *"I Did Us,"* have already tasted this future. They've faced the challenge of leaving the familiar behind and have experienced the blessings of growth. Their testimonies inspire us to trust God's call, even when the path forward feels uncertain.

Breaking the Fear of the Unknown

Fear often accompanies growth. The future, by its very nature, is unknown, and stepping into it requires courage. But the *"I Did Us"* voices remind us that fear is not the end—it's a barrier to overcome. They've faced their own fears and emerged stronger, proving that the road ahead, while challenging, is worth traveling.

God places these guides in our lives to show us that fear can be defeated. Their experiences teach us that the unknown is not something to be avoided but embraced. When we trust the wisdom of those who've gone before us, we gain the courage to face our fears and step into the fullness of God's purpose.

Consider the story of Ruth. She left everything familiar to follow Naomi, embracing a future that was uncertain and intimidating. But Naomi's wisdom—her *"I Did Us"*—guided Ruth to her destiny. Ruth's willingness to trust Naomi's guidance positioned her to become part of the lineage of Christ. Her story reminds us that when we overcome fear and trust the voices God places in our lives, we step into a purpose far greater than we could imagine.

Facing the Limits of the Past to Step Into the Future

Breaking free from past limits isn't just about moving forward—it's about recognizing and rejecting the patterns that have held us back. The *"I Did Us"* figures in our lives teach us that each new stage requires intentionality and faith. They show us how to break free from mindsets, habits, and relationships that no longer align with God's purpose.

This process of breaking free is not easy, but it is necessary. Just as a seed must break open to grow, we must be willing to endure discomfort and change to reach our next level. The people who say, *"I Did Us,"* have already endured this process. They've learned to trust God's plan and let go of the past, and they stand ready to guide us through the same journey.

Moving Beyond Fear and Embracing Mastery

When we break free from the past, we position ourselves for mastery. Mastery is not about perfection; it's about learning to navigate new challenges with wisdom and confidence. The *"I Did Us"* voices in our lives teach us how to approach these challenges with faith, reminding us that God's plan is always greater than our fears.

As we embrace growth, we prepare ourselves to become someone else's *"I Did Us."* Our own journey of overcoming fear and breaking through limitations equips us to guide others. The scars we bear and the lessons we've learned become the tools that help others navigate their own paths.

Becoming Someone's "I Did Us"

Breaking free from past limits is not just a personal journey—it's a preparation for legacy. As we learn to trust God and embrace growth, we position ourselves to guide others through similar transitions. The people who've said, *"I Did Us,"* remind us that our growth is not just for us—it's for the generations that will follow.

When someone asks for guidance, we can say, *"I've been where you are. I've faced the fear, endured the challenges, and broken through the limits of my past. Let me show you the way."* This is the essence of the *"I Did Us"* legacy—using our experiences to empower others to move forward.

Conclusion: Running Toward the Future With Confidence

The future is calling, and God has prepared something greater than what we've left behind. The *"I Did Us"* voices remind us that we don't have to face the unknown alone. We can lean on their wisdom and trust that God's plan is perfect.

As we step into the future, we honor those who've sacrificed for us, and we prepare ourselves to become a legacy for others. Growth requires leaving the past behind, facing our fears, and embracing the new stages God has designed. When we do, we not only fulfill our own purpose but also inspire and guide others to do the same.

One day, someone will look at us and say, *"You did it for us. You made the way easier for me."* And in that moment, we will know that the legacy of *"I Did Us"* is alive and well.

Chapter 6: Surrendering the Right to Be Right – The Power of Humility

The Trap of Pride

One of the greatest obstacles on the path to purpose is pride. Pride is subtle, often disguising itself as confidence or self-assuredness. Yet, at its core, pride tells us that we don't need help, that we know best, and that we're capable of doing everything on our own. The Bible warns us about the dangers of pride, saying, "Pride goes before destruction, a haughty spirit before a fall" (Proverbs 16:18). Pride creates a barrier between us and others, between us and God, and ultimately between us and our purpose.

When pride enters our hearts, it clouds our judgment, making us less receptive to wisdom, guidance, and correction. It convinces us that we're always right, that we don't need to listen to others, and that we don't need God's help. But the path to becoming somebody's "I Did Us"—the answer and solution for someone else—requires humility. It requires surrendering the need to always be right, the need to always have the last word, and the need to assert our way over God's.

Humility is not a sign of weakness; it's a posture of strength and surrender. It's the recognition that we are always learning, that we are part of something larger than ourselves, and that we don't have all the answers. True humility is the foundation of growth and wisdom. It allows us to learn from those who have gone before us, to receive guidance from those who are wiser, and to ultimately become the people God created us to be.

Learning to Let Go of Being Right

Surrendering the right to be right is not easy, especially when we feel that we are justified or knowledgeable. But being somebody's "I Did Us" often requires us to step back from our own ego. There will be moments when we need to listen rather than speak, to understand rather than argue, and to receive rather than teach. True surrender means choosing humility even when we feel we have a right to assert ourselves.

Jesus Himself exemplified this. Although He was the Son of God, He humbled Himself, taking on human form and serving others. Philippians 2:6-7 says, "Who, being in very nature God, did not consider equality with God something to be used to his own advantage; rather, he made himself nothing by taking the very nature of a servant." Jesus could have asserted His power, His knowledge, and His authority in every situation, but instead, He chose humility. He chose to serve rather than to demand honor, to listen rather than to justify, and to surrender rather than to insist on His own way.

If Jesus, who had every right to assert His authority, chose the path of humility, how much more are we called to surrender the need to be right? When we hold onto pride, we close ourselves off from growth and from the opportunity to serve others effectively. True humility allows us to become the answer that someone else needs, not because we know everything, but because we are open, teachable, and willing to let go of ourselves for the greater good.

Pride and the Fall: Why Surrender is Essential

The Bible is filled with examples of how pride leads to downfall. In the Garden of Eden, Adam and Eve's pride led them to believe they knew better than God, that they could make decisions apart from His guidance. Their pride separated them from God and led to a fall that affected generations. Pride blinds us to truth, convincing us that our way is better, our knowledge is sufficient, and our understanding is complete.

To become somebody's "I Did Us," we have to surrender pride completely. We can't help others effectively if we are focused on preserving our own image, reputation, or sense of superiority. Humility allows us to connect with others on a deeper level, to empathize with their struggles, and to serve without expecting anything in return. When we let go of pride, we become vessels through which God's wisdom and love can flow to those around us.

For many of us, the struggle to surrender pride is an ongoing battle. We may feel we have to be the one with the answers, the one who knows best, the one who is always in control. But this mindset creates walls, not bridges. It prevents us from truly connecting with others, from receiving the wisdom of those who have walked the road before us, and from becoming the answer someone else needs. Pride isolates us, but humility connects us.

Someone Else is Your Opportunity

Just as we are called to serve others with humility, we are also called to receive from others with humility. Sometimes, God sends people into our lives to be our "I Did Us"—to share their wisdom, their experiences, and their hard-earned knowledge. They have already made the mistakes, endured the trials, and learned the lessons. When they come to share what they've gained, it's an opportunity for us to grow without paying the same price they paid.

But if we're filled with pride, we will miss these opportunities. We'll assume we know better, that we have nothing to learn, and that their experiences don't apply to us. In doing so, we close ourselves off from valuable knowledge and insight. The pride that tells us we don't need help blinds us to the blessings God is trying to bring into our lives through others.

Proverbs 11:2 says, "When pride comes, then comes disgrace, but with humility comes wisdom." When we surrender pride, we open ourselves to receive wisdom from others. Whether it's a mentor, a family member, or even a stranger, we must recognize that God places people in our lives who have already walked the road we're on. Their insights can save us time, prevent unnecessary mistakes, and guide us toward the fulfillment of our purpose.

Bought Sense: The Wisdom of Those Who've Gone Before

There's an old saying that "bought sense is the best kind of sense." It means that the knowledge we pay for through experience, through trials, and through sacrifice, is knowledge we won't soon forget. It becomes part of who we are. Many of us know this kind of "bought sense" in our own lives—the wisdom we've gained because we went through something challenging and came out stronger, wiser, and more resilient.

But here's the beauty of humility: we don't always have to learn through our own mistakes. God often places people in our lives who have already paid the price, who have already endured the hardships, and who are now willing to share what they've learned with us. These people are our "I Did Us"—they are the ones who come to offer us guidance and direction based on their hard-earned experiences.

If we're humble enough to listen, we can gain "bought sense" without paying the same price. We can learn from others' experiences, from their mistakes, and from their victories. But if pride blinds us, we'll dismiss their wisdom, thinking we don't need it. We'll miss the opportunity to learn, to grow, and to avoid pitfalls. Humility allows us to receive the wisdom of others with gratitude, understanding that God is using their journey to shape ours.

Pride in Receiving: Missing Out on God's Gifts Through Others

When someone comes into our life offering wisdom, knowledge, or support, they are a gift from God. They are positioned to help us, to show us the way, and to save us from unnecessary struggles. But if we're filled with pride, we may reject this gift, thinking we don't need their help. We may assume we know best, that we don't need anyone's advice, and that we're capable of handling things on our own.

This kind of pride is a barrier to growth. If God is sending someone into our life to be an "I Did Us" for us, to guide and mentor us, and we reject their wisdom out of pride, we miss out on what God is trying to impart. We're called to be teachable, to recognize that there is always more to learn, and to receive the gifts of knowledge and wisdom that others bring.

In 1 Peter 5:5, we are reminded, "God opposes the proud but shows favor to the humble." When we choose humility, we align ourselves with God's favor. We position ourselves to receive the blessings and guidance He has placed in our path. Pride, on the other hand, closes us off from these blessings, isolating us from the very people God has sent to help us.

Becoming the Answer Through Humility

Surrendering the right to be right isn't just about giving up our pride; it's about embracing humility as a path to purpose. When we choose humility, we open ourselves to learn, to grow, and to become the answer that someone else needs. Jesus demonstrated this humility throughout His life. He knew He was right, but He didn't assert His knowledge or demand recognition. Instead, He served, loved, and taught with gentleness and patience.

As we let go of pride, we position ourselves to fulfill our purpose with authenticity and grace. We become vessels through which God's wisdom, love, and guidance can flow. Whether we are receiving wisdom from others or sharing what we have learned, humility allows us to be effective, to connect deeply with others, and to serve in a way that leaves a lasting impact.

Pride tells us to hold on to control, to demand our way, and to refuse help. Humility, however, releases these demands, surrendering our lives to God's plan and recognizing the value of others in our journey. As we surrender the right to be right, we become the solution, the "I Did Us" that someone else is searching for. And in the same way, we become receptive to the solutions God is placing in our path through others.

Let us choose humility, letting go of pride, and embracing the opportunities God brings through both our journey and the journeys of others. By doing so, we fulfill our purpose, not through self-assuredness, but through the surrendered strength of humility.

Chapter 7: Enduring Through the Waiting – Trusting God's Timing

The Waiting Room of Life

Life is filled with seasons of waiting, times when we've done everything we can and are left to sit patiently, trusting that the outcome will be worth the wait. Waiting can be challenging, even exhausting. But it is often during these seasons that we experience some of the most profound growth. God uses waiting to strengthen our faith, refine our character, and prepare us for the purpose He has planned.

Think of a family awaiting the birth of a baby. The mother has carried her child for nine long months, enduring discomfort, pain, and anticipation. Family members and friends share in the anticipation, eagerly awaiting the day when they'll meet the new addition. But as eager as everyone is, there's nothing they can do to rush the process. The baby will arrive at the appointed time and not a moment sooner. Despite the anticipation, the timing is out of their control, and all they can do is wait.

This waiting period is a test of patience for everyone involved. The mother may feel uncomfortable, ready to have her body back, and the family may be anxious to hold the new baby. But each person must come to terms with the fact that no amount of eagerness, impatience, or even medical intervention can speed up the timing if the baby isn't ready to be born. There's a time set for all things, including birth, and the natural process must unfold as it is intended.

The Growing Discomfort of Waiting

During the final weeks of pregnancy, many mothers feel a profound sense of discomfort and exhaustion. They're ready to "put the baby down," as some say, wanting nothing more than to be relieved of the physical strain. The weight of carrying life, the sleepless nights, the aches and pains—all of it seems endless. The waiting feels unbearable, and yet, no matter what they do, they cannot rush the arrival of their child.

This physical and emotional tension mirrors the waiting periods we all face in life. Whether we're waiting for a dream to come to fruition, for a breakthrough in a difficult season, or for a long-awaited answer to prayer, we often find ourselves weary and impatient. We feel the discomfort of waiting, eager for relief, wishing we could somehow speed up the process. We might even try to "induce" the outcome ourselves, looking for shortcuts or pushing forward in our own strength. But just as the timing of a birth is beyond our control, so too are the timings of God's plans for our lives.

The Moment of Manifestation

After months of waiting, the time finally arrives. Labor begins, and the family rushes to the hospital. The moment they've all anticipated is at hand. When the baby is born, there's an overwhelming sense of relief, joy, and awe. The mother holds her newborn on her chest, feeling a love she couldn't have imagined. In that moment, all the discomfort, waiting, and anticipation melt away, replaced by the joy of finally holding the promise in her arms.

This is what it feels like when God's timing aligns, when the season of waiting gives way to the manifestation of His promise. In those moments, we look back on all the trials, the pain, and the weariness, realizing that it was all part of the journey. Just as the mother's pain and patience were necessary to bring new life into the world, our own waiting seasons are necessary to bring forth the purposes God has planted in us.

When we finally see the outcome of our waiting, we can appreciate everything that led to it. We understand that the process was not in vain, that every moment of discomfort and impatience was preparing us to receive the promise fully. Just as the joy of a newborn in her arms helps a mother forget the pains of labor, the fulfillment of God's promises in our lives eclipses the hardships we endured in the waiting.

God's Test of Trust

In seasons of waiting, God is doing more than simply making us wait. He's testing our trust in Him, refining our character, and preparing us for what lies ahead. Waiting teaches us to lean not on our own understanding, but on His wisdom and timing. God wants to know that we will remain faithful even when we can't see His hand moving. He wants to be sure that we'll stay steady in our faith, trusting that He is at work, even when we can't perceive it.

James 1:4 reminds us, "Let perseverance finish its work so that you may be mature and complete, not lacking anything." Waiting builds resilience, patience, and maturity in us. It teaches us to be steadfast, to trust that God is working behind the scenes, and to believe that His timing is always perfect. He wants to see that we're willing to endure, that we won't fall apart or give up every time we're asked to wait.

In the waiting room of life, God asks us to trust Him deeply. He wants to know that our faith is grounded, that we can persevere without constantly needing reassurance. Just as a mother endures the final, uncomfortable weeks of pregnancy, knowing that the outcome is worth the wait, we must learn to endure with hope, believing that God's promise will come to fruition in His perfect timing.

The Danger of Rushing the Process

There are times when we, like an impatient mother, attempt to rush the process. We want to induce our "labor," to bring forth the outcome before it's ready. But rushing God's timing often leads to disappointment, frustration, and, in some cases, failure. When we step outside of God's timing, we're not prepared for the responsibilities that come with the blessing. Just as a premature birth carries risks, an attempt to force God's hand can leave us unprepared and vulnerable.

Ecclesiastes 3:1 reminds us, "There is a time for everything, and a season for every activity under the heavens." God's timing is purposeful. He knows when we're ready to receive His promises and when we need more preparation. Our impatience can't change His plans. The best we can do is to trust that He knows what He's doing and that His timing is for our good.

When we try to take matters into our own hands, we risk missing out on God's best for us. We may end up settling for less than what He intended, simply because we couldn't wait. Trusting God's timing requires surrender, a willingness to say, "I'll wait for Your perfect plan, even if it's uncomfortable." Just as a mother cannot rush her baby's development, we cannot rush God's work in our lives.

Becoming Somebody's "I Did Us" Through the Waiting

The season of waiting is not just about us; it's about the people we are called to serve. When we wait faithfully, enduring the discomfort and trusting God's timing, we become stronger, wiser, and more resilient. These qualities are not only for our benefit—they are the very traits we need to become somebody's "I Did Us."

When God finally brings the promise to pass, when He places the "baby" in our arms, we are better prepared to steward it well. We have gained patience, maturity, and faith that will sustain us and those we are called to impact. Just as a mother's love for her newborn is enriched by the struggles of pregnancy, our ability to serve and support others is deepened by the struggles we endure in our waiting seasons.

If we rush through or try to escape these waiting periods, we miss out on the lessons and growth that God intends for us. We may end up unprepared to fulfill the purpose He has set before us. But if we surrender, trusting that God is using this time to shape us, we emerge as stronger vessels, ready to be the answer for someone else.

Learning Patience Through the Journey

In our modern world, waiting is rarely appreciated. We live in a culture of instant gratification, where we expect quick solutions and immediate results. But God's timing doesn't operate on our schedule. When He asks us to wait, it's an invitation to slow down, to trust, and to allow Him to work in ways we may not understand.

Like the expectant mother waiting for her child to arrive, we must learn to embrace the process, even when it's uncomfortable. The journey teaches us patience, humility, and reliance on God. In those final, weary weeks of waiting, the mother may feel ready to give up, but she knows that the birth of her child is close. Similarly, in our waiting seasons, God wants us to hold on, to trust that the fulfillment of His promise is near, and that the journey is worth it.

Trusting God When We Can't See the Finish Line

Waiting requires faith, especially when we can't see how long the journey will last. God doesn't always reveal the timing of His plans, and this can be challenging. But He calls us to trust Him, to believe that He knows the end from the beginning. Isaiah 40:31 promises, "But those who hope in the Lord will renew their strength. They will soar on wings like eagles; they will run and not grow weary, they will walk and not be faint."

God renews our strength as we wait on Him, as we choose to trust that He's in control. Our faith is strengthened in the waiting, as we learn to lean not on our own understanding but on His wisdom and timing. The waiting is not wasted. Every moment we spend trusting Him, every day we endure with patience, is preparing us for the fulfillment of His promise.

The Reward of Endurance

When the promise finally arrives, when the season of waiting is over, the reward is often greater than we imagined. Just as the mother forgets the pains of labor when she holds her newborn, we too are filled with joy and gratitude when God's timing finally aligns with our desires. We look back on the journey with appreciation, realizing that every struggle, every prayer, and every moment of waiting was necessary.

Our endurance in the waiting room of life prepares us to be somebody's "I Did Us." It strengthens our faith, sharpens our character, and fills us with the resilience we need to support and guide others. God's timing is not just about giving us what we want; it's about shaping us into the people we're called to be, ready to carry the weight of the blessings He has prepared for us.

As we endure, we are reminded that every season has a purpose, and that God's timing is always perfect. Our waiting is not in vain, and when the time is right, He will fulfill His promise, bringing forth the "baby" He has planted within us, to bless not only our lives but the lives of those around us.

Chapter 8: Finding Strength in God's Silence – Trusting the "I Did Us" in the Quiet

Introduction: Trusting God and His "I Did Us" in the Quiet Moments
There are times in life when God seems silent, and the absence of a clear word or direction feels overwhelming. In these moments, we're left to navigate uncertainty, wondering why He isn't saying or doing something. Yet, it is often in these quiet seasons that God invites us to find strength—not in answers, but in the silence itself.

Just as others have walked this road before us and found clarity in the quiet, we must trust that God's silence is not abandonment but preparation. The "I Did Us" of faith in silence is reflected in those who have learned to say, *"When God is silent, I will trust Him anyway."* They've walked through seasons of uncertainty, returning to His last word, remembering His past faithfulness, and leaning into the assurance that He will never leave or forsake us.

The Strength of Trust Built on the Faithfulness of Others

Trust is not just a personal journey—it's one that builds on the examples of those who've gone before us. Think of the "I Did Us" figures in your life—those who've endured silent seasons and emerged with unwavering faith. They've trusted God when He seemed quiet, and their stories remind us that silence is not absence. When you hear their testimonies, they often say, *"I've been there, and I can tell you, God was working even when I couldn't hear Him."*

Their faith is built on trust forged in the fire of silence. When God seems silent, they remind us to look back at the last thing He said, to remember His faithfulness, and to trust that He is still present. Their scars and stories become a guide, showing us how to endure silence with grace and faith.

Returning to God's Last Word

In the quiet, God may not give us new instructions because He's already spoken what we need to know for this moment. Silence isn't rejection—it's a sign that He trusts us to follow what He's already given. Many "I Did Us" voices will tell you, *"When God seems silent, go back to His last word and hold on to it."*

When you're unsure, revisit the promises He's already fulfilled in your life. Think of the times He came through when you thought all was lost. This is the essence of trust—returning to what you know is true, even when circumstances tempt you to doubt. The legacy of "I Did Us" reminds us that God's silence doesn't mean His absence; it's an opportunity to deepen our faith and refine our patience.

Memory as a Trust Anchor

Memory is a powerful anchor in the midst of silence. Those who say, *"I Did Us,"* often tell us to reflect on the ways God has moved in the past. Think of Joseph, who endured years of silence in prison. He had to remember the dreams God gave him and trust that those dreams would be fulfilled in time. Joseph's story is a testament to the strength of trusting God in the quiet, holding onto His last word, and believing that silence does not mean forgotten.

When you're in the silence, recall the faithfulness of God not only in your own life but in the lives of others who've gone before you. Their stories become a source of strength, reminding you that you're not alone and that silence is often the prelude to God's greatest moves.

The Role of "I Did Us" in Silent Seasons

Silent seasons are not just personal tests—they're also moments that prepare you to be someone else's "I Did Us." When you endure silence and learn to trust God, you gain a depth of faith and wisdom that becomes invaluable to others. When someone else feels abandoned or unsure, you can say, *"I've been there. I know it's hard, but I also know God is faithful. He's working, even when it feels like He's far away."*

The silence you endure now equips you to help others in their silent seasons. Your ability to trust God when He's quiet becomes a testimony that reassures and strengthens others. When you say, *"I Did Us,"* you're offering the gift of encouragement, a reminder that silence is not the end of the story.

Releasing the Need for Immediate Answers

Many of us struggle with silence because we crave immediate answers. But as we grow in faith, we learn to let go of the need for constant reassurance. We come to a place where we can say, *"Even if I can't hear Him right now, I know He's here."* This release is a hallmark of maturity—it's what allows us to walk by faith, not by sight or sound.

When others see this kind of faith in you, it becomes a witness to the power of trust. Your ability to rest in God's faithfulness during silence teaches them that they, too, can find strength in the quiet. This is the legacy of "I Did Us"—a legacy of trust that passes from one person to another, inspiring faith in the midst of uncertainty.

Conclusion: Strength in Silence and the Call to Share It

Finding strength in God's silence is one of the most profound lessons we can learn. It's a lesson built on trust, memory, and the assurance that God is always present, even when He's not speaking. Those who've walked this road before us—those who've endured silent seasons and come out stronger—offer us the gift of their testimony. They remind us that silence is not abandonment but preparation.

As you navigate your own silent seasons, remember that you're not just enduring for yourself. You're being equipped to be someone else's "I Did Us." Your faith, forged in the silence, will one day be the anchor someone else needs when they face their own quiet moments.

And when that day comes, you'll be able to look at them with confidence and say, *"I've been there. I endured the silence. And I can tell you this: God is faithful."*

Chapter 9: Positioned to Receive – Embracing God's Provision Through Others

Recognizing Divine Help When It Arrives

In our journeys, God often sends people into our lives who have walked the roads we're on, who have faced similar trials, and who have gained wisdom through experience. These people come with insight, support, and answers that can help us avoid mistakes, gain clarity, and grow in ways we couldn't on our own. Yet, there's a challenge: to receive what they bring, we have to let go of our doubts, our need for control, and our pride. We have to be willing to believe that God is using others to bless us, guide us, and help us reach our purpose.

It's easy to miss the help God sends if we're focused on doing everything ourselves or if we don't recognize the value others bring. But part of being somebody's "I Did Us" is also learning how to receive from those who are willing to share their "I Did Us" moments with us. When someone comes into our lives with hard-earned wisdom, we have the opportunity to grow if we're willing to listen, learn, and receive.

Letting Go of Doubt and Embracing God's Provision

When we doubt the value of others' experiences or question whether they can truly help us, we close ourselves off from the blessings God has prepared. It's tempting to think, I can handle this on my own, or No one knows my situation as well as I do. But doubt prevents us from fully receiving the wisdom and support others offer. James 1:6-7 reminds us that "when you ask, you must believe and not doubt, because the one who doubts is like a wave of the sea, blown and tossed by the wind. That person should not expect to receive anything from the Lord."

To receive from God through others, we have to trust that He knows what we need and that He may send people into our lives to provide it. When we let go of doubt, we open ourselves to the idea that God's help doesn't always come directly from Him—it often comes through the people He places around us.

Being Willing to Listen and Learn

There's an important difference between hearing someone's advice and truly listening to it. When God places someone in our life to share their wisdom, it's not enough to simply nod politely. We must open our hearts and minds, taking the time to listen carefully and consider what they're saying. Proverbs 19:20 tells us, "Listen to advice and accept discipline, and at the end you will be counted among the wise."

Listening requires humility, patience, and an openness to learn. It means setting aside our own assumptions and truly hearing what the other person is offering. When we listen with an open heart, we allow God's guidance to flow through them and into our lives. We position ourselves to receive insights and encouragement that can help us grow, change, and reach our potential.

Embracing the "I Did Us" of Others

When God sends someone who's already walked through the fire we're facing, who's endured hardships similar to ours, He is offering us a blessing. This person has already done the work, gained the experience, and learned the hard lessons. They come as a gift, a source of wisdom that can save us from unnecessary pain and setbacks.

But pride can block us from receiving this blessing. Pride says, I don't need anyone's help. I can figure it out on my own. Yet God often humbles us by using others to provide the guidance we need. Jesus Himself demonstrated the importance of humility and receiving from others. Although He was the Son of God, He accepted help, guidance, and support from people during His earthly ministry. By humbling ourselves, we acknowledge that we don't know everything and that God may use others to complete our journey.

Imagine how different the story of Elisha's servant would be if he had allowed pride to cloud his vision. In 2 Kings 6:15-17, when Elisha's servant saw enemy armies surrounding them, he was filled with fear. But Elisha prayed, "Open his eyes, Lord, so that he may see." When God opened the servant's eyes, he saw heavenly armies surrounding them, ready to protect them. In that moment, the servant's faith was restored because he saw the divine help he hadn't initially recognized. Sometimes, we too need to pray for God to open our eyes to the help He is sending us through others.

When Receiving Means Trusting the Timing

God's provision often comes in His timing, not ours. Sometimes, we're eager for answers and solutions, but God knows exactly when to send the people we need into our lives. When we're ready to receive, He provides. Just as a mother waits for the right time for her baby to be born, we must trust God's timing in sending us the right people at the right time.

This may mean waiting longer than we'd like or being patient with those God has placed in our lives. Learning from others takes time, and we may not see the full value of their guidance immediately. But if we remain open, willing, and patient, we'll eventually see how their "I Did Us" moments shape our journey.

Recognizing Divine Appointments

Not everyone who comes into our life will be a source of guidance, but some relationships are clearly divine appointments. God often places specific people in our path who can impart exactly what we need to know at a particular stage. When we encounter these people, we need to be receptive, discerning, and willing to embrace what they offer.

Divine appointments are moments where God uses others to help us navigate challenges, open doors, and grow in ways we couldn't on our own. These people may come with hard truths, challenging us to think differently or stretch beyond our comfort zones. They may come with words of encouragement, support, or wisdom that we desperately need. When we recognize these encounters as divinely orchestrated, we can fully embrace the blessing God has provided.

Positioning Yourself to Receive

Positioning ourselves to receive from others requires a mindset shift. We must let go of self-reliance, pride, and doubt, allowing ourselves to be vulnerable and open to what others offer. It means acknowledging that we don't have all the answers and being willing to receive from someone else's journey.

To position ourselves to receive, we need to adopt a posture of humility and gratitude. When someone offers us wisdom or guidance, we should thank God for sending them. We should pray for open hearts and clear minds, asking God to remove any doubts or hesitations that might prevent us from fully receiving what He's providing through others.

The Prayer of Receiving: Opening Our Eyes to God's Provision

At times, it can be difficult to recognize or accept the help God sends through others. Our own doubts, insecurities, or pride can cloud our vision, keeping us from fully receiving the gifts He provides. But we can pray, asking God to open our eyes and remove any blinders that keep us from seeing His hand at work.

A Prayer for Receiving

Heavenly Father, I thank You for the ways You provide for me, even through the lives of others. I acknowledge that sometimes I struggle to receive guidance, to accept help, and to believe that others may hold the wisdom I need. I ask that You would soften my heart, Lord. Remove any pride or doubt that stands in the way of receiving what You are offering.

Lord, I pray that You open my eyes, as You did for Elisha's servant, so I may see the help You've surrounded me with. Remove the veil from my vision, so that I can clearly recognize the people You've placed in my life for this season. Help me to see their "I Did Us" moments as gifts meant to guide and support me.

Father, give me a teachable spirit, one that is willing to listen, learn, and accept wisdom from others. Help me to let go of any need to do things on my own and to trust that You are working through those around me. May I be humble enough to receive, knowing that Your provision sometimes comes through the hands and hearts of others.

Lord, I want to be someone's "I Did Us" as well, so teach me through the experiences of others that I may grow and be prepared to serve others when it is my time. Thank You for every divine appointment, every person who comes into my life to share their journey. I receive them as gifts from You, with gratitude and faith. In Jesus' name, Amen.

Chapter 10: Embracing the Legacy of "I Did Us" and Passing It On

Understanding Your Joseph Moment

When we look back at Joseph's story, we see that everything he endured—betrayal, false accusations, imprisonment, and isolation—had purpose. Each trial refined him and prepared him for the role God had destined him to fill. When Joseph finally stood in a position of power, he was able to look his brothers in the eyes and say, "Am I in the place of God?" (Genesis 50:19). Joseph recognized that his journey had placed him precisely where he needed to be to provide for others, even those who had wronged him.

Reaching our own "Joseph moment" means understanding that all we've gone through is not just for ourselves, but for the people God will place in our lives. The wisdom, resilience, and skills we've gained are not meant to be stored up for our own benefit. They're meant to be poured out, shared, and passed on to others. Embracing the legacy of "I Did Us" is a call to humility, to recognize that the knowledge and experiences we've gained are gifts meant to bless others.

Being Willing to Share

When someone comes to you seeking guidance, they're often at a crossroads, facing decisions or challenges that feel overwhelming. Imagine they're asking, "How do I build a business?" "What does it take to succeed in this field?" "How do I navigate this difficult relationship?" If you've been down that road, your answer holds the power to shape their journey. You have the ability to steer them away from traps, help them avoid costly mistakes, and direct them toward the tools and resources that work best.

But to give this kind of help, you need a heart posture of humility and generosity. You can't hold back the knowledge you've gained out of pride, resentment, or a belief that others should struggle just as you did. Embracing the legacy of "I Did Us" means understanding that our struggles were not wasted. They were investments, not just in ourselves but in others. Holding back what we know out of a "figure it out for yourself" mentality deprives someone else of the opportunity to grow, succeed, and fulfill their purpose.

Embracing the Role of the "I Did Us"

Embracing this role means positioning yourself as a guide, mentor, and servant, willing to help others with the knowledge you've gained. It's about being someone who says, "I did this, and here's what I learned," not as a boast, but as an offering to those who are searching for direction. When you tell someone, "Oh, don't use that platform—it locks you in for months," or "Choose this software because it'll get you better visibility," you're helping them make choices that will set them up for success.

Being the "I Did Us" is like being a well of knowledge that others can draw from. Think of the lessons you've learned, the insights you've gained, and the scars you bear as resources to share. You've already paid the price, made the mistakes, and faced the obstacles. Now, when someone else approaches you, they don't have to pay that same price—you've paid it for them. This is what it means to be an "I Did Us." It's about using your life's experiences to bring others forward and to elevate them.

A Tree that Bears Fruit for Others

Consider a tree that bears fruit. An apple tree does not eat its own apples, nor does a peach tree eat its own peaches. Their fruit is meant for others to enjoy. Likewise, the wisdom, insight, and experience you've gained are the fruits of your life that others can benefit from. Just as a tree produces fruit that feeds others, your life produces knowledge and insight that others can draw from. To embrace the legacy of "I Did Us" is to see yourself as a source of sustenance, offering guidance and wisdom for others on their own journeys.

A singer sings for the enjoyment of others, a musician creates music to uplift and inspire, and a storyteller shares to entertain or enlighten. In the same way, you are called to offer what you have learned as a gift to others. If you have the skills, insights, and knowledge someone else needs, you have an opportunity to enrich their life. It's a call to be generous with what God has given you, knowing that when you share, you multiply the impact of what you've learned.

Passing It On with Humility and Gratitude

When you have embraced the legacy of "I Did Us," you become a bridge for others to cross over from uncertainty to clarity, from confusion to direction. But this legacy requires a heart willing to serve. Many people hold back what they know out of fear, pride, or insecurity. They might think, I had to learn this the hard way, so should you. But a heart that's willing to pass on wisdom is a heart that God can use for greater things.

Your journey wasn't just for you—it was for those who would come after you. When you share your knowledge, you're participating in God's work of empowering others. You're sowing seeds of wisdom that will bear fruit in someone else's life. Just as someone may have been there for you in a moment of need, guiding you with their hard-earned wisdom, you now have the privilege to pass that on.

What It Means to Embrace the Legacy

To truly embrace the legacy of "I Did Us" means living with an open hand. It's a commitment to give back, to be a willing vessel of God's wisdom and provision for others. Embracing this legacy means being able to look at someone who's struggling and say, "Here, let me help. I've been there, and this is what I've learned." It's about letting go of any pride or reservations that might hold you back from sharing and serving.

Living with the "I Did Us" mindset also means remaining humble, knowing that everything you've learned was given by God and that He can use it to bless others. Just as Joseph realized that his trials were meant to save lives, you can see that your experiences were not just for you. They were for those God would send your way, those who would benefit from the road you've already traveled.

Stepping into the Role of a Guide

As you continue on your journey, pray for God to open your eyes to those who need your guidance, those who are searching for answers you already hold. Ask Him to give you the grace to share what you've learned freely, without reservation, and to recognize the value of every "I Did Us" moment He has given you.

When someone comes to you with questions or struggles, remember the times you were in their shoes. Remember the people who guided you, the mentors who shared their wisdom, and the friends who supported you. Now it's your turn to step into that role, to be a light for someone else, to share your hard-earned knowledge, and to help them navigate their journey.

Ending with a Final Charge

When someone asks you how to navigate a challenge or overcome an obstacle, don't hesitate to share. Guide them, teach them, and encourage them. Show them the lessons you learned, the paths you took, and the insights you gained. Give them what you wished someone had given you. In doing so, you're passing on the legacy of "I Did Us."

Embrace it fully. Live with a heart that's open, a spirit that's willing, and a commitment to help others on their journey. When you do, you'll discover the beauty of a life lived in service, a life that reaches beyond itself to lift others higher.

The Final Word: You, Too, Will One Day Say, "I Did Us."

Remember, you are both the recipient and the giver in this journey. Just as you've been blessed to receive wisdom and guidance, you are now blessed to pass it on. You, too, will one day look back and see the lives you've touched, the hearts you've encouraged, and the people you've helped.

And in that moment, you will be able to say with gratitude and humility, "I did us."

Chapter 11: The Road Less Traveled – Overcoming Fear to Fulfill the Legacy of "I Did Us"

Introduction: The Path Prepared for Me

When I reflect on the journey of becoming someone's *"I Did Us,"* one personal experience comes to mind that profoundly shaped my understanding of obedience, trust, and the cost of fear. Moving into a new home with my family brought me face-to-face with a fear that seemed small at first but revealed itself as a significant spiritual lesson.

God often places us on paths that feel daunting or even impossible to navigate. These paths, while terrifying at times, are designed to shape us and bring us closer to fulfilling His purpose for our lives. However, when we allow fear to dictate our actions, we not only prolong our journey but risk delaying the blessings of those who are waiting on the other side of our obedience. What I learned during this season is that avoiding the road God has prepared doesn't make the journey easier—it makes it longer and far more difficult.

Facing the Mountain

When we first moved into our home, our realtor took us through the most direct route—a narrow, winding mountain pass with steep cliffs and no guardrails. It was breathtakingly beautiful but absolutely terrifying. Looking out the window, it felt like one wrong move could send us over the edge. I gripped the seat so tightly that my hands ached by the time we arrived.

The realtor, who had driven the route many times, navigated it with ease and confidence. But for me, the fear of that road was overwhelming. As soon as we settled into the house, I told my husband, Craig, that I would never drive through those mountains alone. I meant it. In fact, I made him promise that whenever I needed to go somewhere, especially to church—he would drive me.

Taking the Long Way Around

Craig, being the supportive husband he is, agreed, but there were times when his ministry obligations required him to be elsewhere. On those occasions, I had no choice but to drive myself. Rather than face the mountain pass, I decided to take an alternate route—a road that felt safer but added an hour to my drive. Instead of 26 minutes, it took me an hour and 26 minutes to reach my destination. At first, I convinced myself that the longer route was a better choice. It felt safer, even if it was inconvenient.

But then came the mornings when I overslept or underestimated how much time I needed to get ready. Suddenly, that extra hour became a major problem. I'd be rushing out the door, panicking about being late, and speeding down the road. I remember yelling at other drivers, "Why are you going so slow? Get out of my way!" I was so angry at everyone else for moving at their own pace, not realizing that the problem wasn't them, it was me. They were on the road they were supposed to be on, moving at the speed that was appropriate for them. Meanwhile, I was on the wrong road, creating chaos because of my refusal to take the path that had been prepared for me.

The Cost of Fear

Looking back, I realize how much my fear cost me—and how it affected others. Taking the long way around seemed like the safer choice, but it added unnecessary stress, wasted time, and created frustration. More than that, it delayed me from fulfilling my responsibilities in ministry.

One Sunday morning, I arrived late to church, flustered and embarrassed. The team I was serving with had been waiting for me to arrive so we could begin our assignments. They were gracious and understanding, but I knew the truth. My lateness wasn't caused by traffic or unforeseen circumstances, it was because of my own fear.

This realization was humbling. I thought about the times I had prayed for God to use me, to make me a vessel for His kingdom. And yet here I was, allowing fear to hold me back from fulfilling my purpose. I began to see how my delays didn't just affect me—they affected the people God had placed in my life. They were waiting on me to get myself together so that we could move forward together.

Learning to Trust God's Plan

Eventually, I had to confront my fear of the mountain pass. I asked God to help me face it, to give me the courage to trust that He would guide and protect me. The first time I drove through the mountains alone, my heart was pounding, and my hands were shaking. But as I kept driving, something shifted. I realized that the road wasn't as scary as I had made it out to be in my mind. Each time I drove it, I became more confident, until eventually, the fear was gone.

This experience taught me an important lesson about obedience. When God places a road before us, it's because He knows it's the best path to take—even if it looks intimidating. The longer we avoid it, the more time we waste, and the more likely we are to cause unnecessary delays for ourselves and others.

The "I Did Us" Legacy in Action

I think about how this applies to the *"I Did Us"* concept. When we refuse to obey God and take the road He's prepared, we risk holding up the people who are waiting for us to step into our purpose. Just like my ministry team was waiting for me to arrive, there are people in your life who are waiting for you to get where you need to be. They need you to face your fear, trust God, and walk the path He has laid out for you.

At the same time, we must remember that there are people who've gone before us, like my realtor who confidently navigated the mountain pass. These *"I Did Us"* figures are guides, showing us that the road is possible to travel. Their confidence comes from experience—they've faced the fear, endured the challenges, and made it through to the other side. They say to us, *"I did this, and you can too."*

Conclusion: Moving in Sync with God's Plan

As I close this chapter—and this book—I want to encourage you, beloved, to trust the path God has chosen for you. You may not understand every twist and turn, and the road may feel overwhelming at times. But remember this: God's plan is perfect, and every detail has been accounted for. When you let go of fear and fully surrender to His will, you align yourself with His purpose and timing.

There are people waiting for you to step into your role as their *"I Did Us."* Don't let fear or disobedience hold you back. Ask God to help you move in sync with His plan, trusting that He will guide you every step of the way.

To my family in Christ—my spiritual parents, Prophetess Taryn Nicole Tarver Bishop and Apostle Paul Bishop; my spiritual grandfather, Prophet Lovy

Elias; my spiritual grandmother, Prophetess Maggie Elias; and my spiritual great-grandparents, Papa and Mama Passion Java—you have been my first *"I Did Us."* Your love, guidance, and examples have shown me how to walk this road, and for that, I am forever grateful.

Shalom.

Don't miss out!

Visit the website below and you can sign up to receive emails whenever Apostle Paula Ferguson publishes a new book. There's no charge and no obligation.

https://books2read.com/r/B-A-FQUQC-RDUIF

BOOKS 2 READ

Connecting independent readers to independent writers.

Did you love *The "I Did Us" Concept!*? Then you should read *I Just Don't Feel Like It! Finding Motivation When Life Hits Snooze*[1] by Apostle Paula Ferguson!

[2]

There are days when you simply don't feel like *doing anything*. You don't feel like adulting, being a mom or dad, a spouse, sibling, friend, or anything other than *you*. You can't pinpoint the reason, but it feels like every time you try to dive back into life, *life hits the snooze button*.

Guess what? You don't owe anyone an explanation for why you don't feel up to it. But you *do* owe it to yourself to find out *why*. Why is it that, on some days, you just can't seem to move forward?

So, what part of you is speaking—is it your spirit, your soul, or your body? Is it your spirit that's lacking connection with God? Is it your soul, feeling frustrated because something seems to be blocking your path to success? Or is it your body, simply exhausted from the demands of all the roles you play? Who or what part of you is really talking? We are spirit, soul, and body. Are you listening?

---

1. https://books2read.com/u/bQ70VP

2. https://books2read.com/u/bQ70VP

I Just Don't Feel Like It is about more than simply not wanting to be bothered. It's about finding motivation when life would rather hit the snooze button. This book empowers you to understand yourself more deeply. You don't owe anyone an explanation, but you owe it to yourself to find out *why*.

Also by Apostle Paula Ferguson

Fridge Forks and Fresh Starts: "Building a Healthy Kitchen"
I Just Don't Feel Like It! Finding Motivation When Life Hits Snooze
I Will Understanding Your Divine Calling
Make it Make Sense Recognizing the Move of God in Real Time
The "I Did Us" Concept!

About the Author

About the Author – Apostle Paula Ferguson

Apostle Paula Ferguson is a dynamic and prophetic leader with decades of ministry experience, known for her profound wisdom, spiritual insight, and commitment to empowering others. Her mission to inspire the spiritual growth as a necessary part of living a purpose-driven life.

As an advocate for holistic health, Apostle Ferguson believes that taking care of the body is essential for fulfilling God's calling. Her passion for **helping the body of Christ thrive** led her to explore the challenges people face when trying to live a healthy lifestyle. She understands that true transformation happens when we align **spiritual purpose with physical well-being**—starting in the kitchen.

Apostle Ferguson's ministry is marked by testimonies of healing, deliverance, and restoration, and she now extends this gift into the realm of wellness. She equips others with the tools and knowledge needed to overcome the practical challenges of eating well, staying active, and building healthy habits that last. Through her teachings and writings, Apostle Ferguson inspires believers to embrace the connection between **health and purpose**, empowering them to live fully and thrive in every area of life.

About the Publisher

About FOSA Publishing Company

which stands for *Family of Successful Authors*, is a Christian publishing house committed to helping authors share the Gospel of Jesus Christ with ease and efficiency. At FOSA, we believe that bringing the Word of God to others should be an accessible and streamlined process. Inspired by stories of perseverance, like that of Charlie Sifford—who, despite racial barriers, became a successful golfer simply because he "just wanted to play"—we aim to support authors in publishing their messages quickly and effectively. Our mission is to empower writers to reach the body of Christ, sharing transformative messages with a global audience.